KUNG-FU CARP FISHING

by Adam Dailey-McIlrath
FishingDojo.com

Disclaimer and Terms of Use

The author and the publisher do not hold any responsibility for errors, omissions, or interpretation of the subject matter herein, and specifically disclaim any responsibility for the safety or appropriateness of any activities or advice presented in this book. This book is presented for informational purposes only.

© 2014 Iron Ring Publishing. All rights reserved
No part of this publication, including graphics and the written information contained herein, may be quoted, reused, transmitted, or reproduced in any form – electronic, mechanical, photocopy, recording, or otherwise – without prior written permission of the copyright holder.

Table of Contents

WHY CARP? 1
A (NOT NECESSARILY ACCURATE) HISTORY OF CARP FISHING 3
ESSENTIAL FUNDAMENTALS – THE FOUR RINGS 5
   The Ring of Casting 5
   The Ring of Perception 6
   The Ring of Shadows 6
   The Ring of Striking 6
A FREE GIFT FOR YOU 8
WHAT YOU NEED TO KNOW ABOUT TERRAIN 9
   Finding the Best Fishing Spots 9
   Spotting Carp 12
FISHING WEAPONS 14
   The Right Gear 14
   You Are Smarter Than The Fish. Or Are You? 15
   Preparing Your Body For The Fight 16
   Choosing The Right Weapons 17
   So You Want To Tie Your Own Flies? 19
      The Shaolin Fireball 19
      The Little Dragon 21
      Dry Flies 23
BOATS 25
WADING AND KUNG-FU FOOTWORK 28
   How To Stalk Carp 28
   Kung-Fu Footwork 29
VITAL TECHNIQUES 31
   The Basics 31
   The Strike 34
   Drawing Your Prey 35
   Seeing Without Seeing 36
   The Heron Technique 38

Fishing Like The Old Master *40*
Landing The Carp *42*
Whispering *43*
The Most Important Thing *44*

About The Author **45**

WHY CARP?

When people talk about fly fishing, they are almost always talking about trout. Sure, there are other fish out there. A few people fly fish for bass or pike, and those lucky anglers that inhabit the coasts can pursue salt water species as well. But trout are the crown jewel of the fly fishing world. They are strikingly colorful fish that swim in some of the most rare and beautiful water in the world, and their shy nature and selective feeding habits make them an excellent challenge for anglers.

Every once in awhile you will run across someone who fly-fishes for carp. These rogue anglers are usually eccentric individuals and are considered crazy (or heretics) by the rest of the fly fishing world. These maniacs are always incredibly excited about carp, and if you listen to them carefully you may begin to wonder if it isn't the trout fishermen who are crazy.

Carp, unlike trout, are accessible to everyone. They can tolerate low levels of oxygen, high levels of pollution and turbidity, and a wide range of temperatures. Because of their toughness you will find them everywhere: in trout streams, northern lakes, southern reservoirs, meandering rivers, urban sloughs and duck ponds. Yet despite their ubiquity, they are smart and spooky fish which require great skill to catch. They also grow quickly and become huge (while trout are measured in inches, carp are measured in pounds).

Outside of saltwater, carp are the only gamefish that regularly require the angler to see the fish before they catch it. This type of "sight-fishing" is incredibly addictive – the instant rush of adrenaline you feel when a fish tugs on your line is drawn out into a rush that starts as soon as you see the carp, and peaks when you actually watch it take your fly.

Carp fishing is also dangerously exciting. I'll never forget, during the thrill of fighting a big carp, suddenly realizing that I was standing in a lake holding a nine foot rod into the air in the middle of a thunderstorm!

Finally, carp are handsome fish that are beautifully adapted to thrive in a variety of habitats. So why don't more people fly fish for carp? Indeed, why doesn't everyone? It is because fly fishing for carp is a carefully guarded secret.

A (NOT NECESSARILY ACCURATE) HISTORY OF CARP FISHING

The art of Kung-Fu Carp Fishing was developed in ancient times by warrior monks. Through intense mental and physical training their bodies became like blocks of iron, their hands like deadly claws, their feet like sledgehammers. After decades of beating down anyone foolish enough to bother them, these monks ended up with a lot of free time, so they started fishing. They quickly realized that among all fishes, the carp was the ultimate, peerless opponent, and so the monks began to develop and refine their carp fishing techniques.

This knowledge has been passed down through the centuries in secret. Indeed, to preserve their art and protect their secrets, it would not be untrue to claim that the adherents of Kung-Fu Carp Fishing have happily encouraged and perpetuated what has become the idolatry of trout by modern fly fishers.

But just as Yip Man finally shared the hidden knowledge of Wing Chun with the world, the time has come for the secrets of Kung-Fu Carp Fishing to be revealed. So just like Old Master passed the knowledge of Kung-Fu Carp Fishing on to me, I am prepared to pass his teachings on to you.

Before you can start hooking up and having fun, there are some things to consider. Catching carp is hard. Catching carp on the fly is harder. If Kung-Fu Carp Fishing were easy, the great enlightened masters of the past would not have bothered. So before we go any further you should learn the first tenet of Kung-Fu Carp Fishing: *Perseverance*.

If you fly fish for carp you will be frustrated, you will be disappointed, you will hurl unintelligible curses at the heavens. But if you fly fish for carp the Kung-Fu way then you will take a deep breath, pick up your rod, and keep on fishing.

If you are willing to accept the first tenet of Kung-Fu Carp Fishing; if you are determined to be an indomitable Kung-Fu angler, then let's get started.

ESSENTIAL FUNDAMENTALS: THE FOUR RINGS

In martial arts – and in fishing – there are fundamental principles of each style, each with its own conceptual framework which is based on certain principles and upon which its techniques are developed. The conceptual framework of Kung-Fu Carp Fishing is **The Book of Four Rings**: the Ring of Casting, the Ring of Perception, the Ring of Shadows and the Ring of Striking. These are not techniques, they are ideas, but every Kung-Fu Carp Fishing technique is based on them. So every time you learn something new or apply something you have learned, do it with the Four Rings you'll learn about below. This will help you develop your style of catching carp, and someday it will help you to pass down the skills of Kung-Fu Carp Fishing to your own students.

The Ring of Casting

The Ring of Casting is known to every fly fisher. You are the center of the ring and its radius is the distance you can cast. Do not let your mind get caught in this ring for that is the mind of the braggart. Too many people are trapped in this ring:

"I can cast X feet"
"I can make an X foot whippy-whirl cast"
"I can make that cast into a Y mile per hour headwind"

These people are not fly fishers. They are fly casters. They have forgotten that the purpose of fishing (which includes casting) is to catch fish. When you understand this distinction you will not be intimidated by their dancing rod tips and fancy loops.

The Ring of Perception

The Ring of Perception is not consciously realized by most fly fishers but it is more important than the Ring of Casting. The Ring of Perception is also centered on you, but its radius is the furthest distance that you can perceive a carp in the water. When you are sight-fishing, the radius of your Ring of Perception effectively limits how far you can cast. If you can only spot the wiley carp at 30 feet, you'll never catch him 32 feet away, no matter how far you can cast! And if you are not sight-fishing then you may as well give up and go catch trout.

The radius of your Ring of Perception depends on the sun, the clouds, the wind, the water and the mood of the gods. The only way to improve your perception is through years and years of dedication and experience ... or you can go buy some polarized sunglasses.

The Ring of Shadows

The carp fears one enemy above all others: the eagle. That is why the biggest, wisest carp always stay near the protection of dense cover or deep water. No matter how intently a carp appears to be feeding or how lazily it seems to be swimming, it is always hyper-alert for the darting shadow of the enemy. The Ring of Shadows is the area that a carp is scanning for danger, and if it senses anything out of the ordinary, you will not catch it.

The Ring of Striking

This is the smallest but most essential Ring of carp fishing. It is a circle centered just in front of a carp's head, like a big bowl of noodles, and it is where you must put your fly if you want the carp to eat it. The radius of this ring is not fixed. If the water is clear, the Ring of Striking will be bigger than when visibility is limited. If the water is warm and the fish are active, they might chase a fly farther. As a rule of thumb, you can figure that this Ring is at least three feet in diameter. This is not a very big target, but it is always better to underestimate.

The four rings are not separated, nor are they tangled around one another. They are fixed but shifting, related but changing, simple yet subtle. The circles must be learned individually but applied together. This is the essence of the four rings of carp fishing.

A FREE GIFT FOR YOU

SEVEN SECRETS OF BASS FISHING.
(FishingDojo.com presents)

If you've read this far, you are clearly a serious fisher who is interested in improving your skills and your experience. As a Thank You for your interest and your confidence, I'd like to give you a free report:

7 Secrets of Bass Fishing

Get it for free right now at
FishingDojo.com!

WHAT YOU NEED TO KNOW ABOUT TERRAIN

"Knowing the place and the time of the coming battle, we may concentrate from the greatest distances in order to fight."

— Sun Tzu, *The Art of War*

The way of Kung-Fu Carp Fishing is simple: it is to catch carp on the fly. But to catch a carp, you must first find one. Thus it is essential to study terrain. Even though carp can live in almost any body of fresh water, the only spots of interest to the fisherman are the ones where he has a chance to catch one.

Finding the Best Fishing Spots

Look for areas with two important attributes: **shallow water** and **good access**.

Using the Ring of Perception (sight-fishing) requires that the area be shallow enough to see feeding fish. Wading requires that the area is shallow enough for you to... well, wade.

The importance of good access is often underrated, but a pond full of carp doesn't do you any good if it is beyond the high fences of some exclusive country club. Pay attention to parking spots, public rights of way, and signs reading "Trespassers will be shot."

There are two techniques that can be employed, alone or together, to find new carp fishing spots: Spying and Scouting.

Spying means gathering information about a place without going there yourself. When it comes to lesser arts like fishing for trout, the traditional approach is to head down to the local fly shop and ask them where to fish. However, if you walk into a fly shop and announce that you fish for carp it is very likely that you will be insulted or laughed at. Then you will have to bust out your Kung-Fu. I recommend the osprey-claws-eyes technique for dealing with trout snobs, and the shark-bites-leg technique against salt water anglers.

Even if you find other carp fishers, they may be secretive and hesitant to share information. In either case you will need to use a different approach: First, pour yourself a good cup of coffee. Next, sit down with an accurate map of the water-body you want to fish. A good map should include water depths and underwater structure. Look for large shallow areas. The larger the area, the more likely part or all of it will be wadable. Sharp bends and feeder streams are good areas to investigate because they often promote the build-up of sediment into fishable flats. Also, note any nearby channels or depressions because carp like to be close to deeper water where they can rest or take cover.

Once you have identified potential fishing spots on the map it is time to scout them out. Scouting means physically exploring a potential spot. Scouting an area before fishing it gives you a big advantage. Familiarity with the terrain means that you will find carp quickly and more consistently when you fish. It also allows you to move freely and confidently over otherwise hazardous terrain.

Many fishers do not think much of scouting an area. They think "Why scout an area when you could just try fishing it?" Of course, by the time such a fair-weather angler wanders into new territory for the first time, a dedicated student of Kung-Fu Carp Fishing has already scouted the spot - he knows every drop-off, every submerged stump and every rock. He even knows some of the local carp by name. To be like him you must train constantly.

You should start scouting potential carp flats in the middle of winter, when the carp are hibernating in deep water and most amateur fishermen are watching football on the couch. This is especially effective in reservoirs that draw down in the winter, exposing the exact shallow areas you are interested in. It is also safer to wander new shorelines in the winter when the poison oak and ivy have died back. Then in the spring when those same shorelines are impassable, you can wade back to exploit what you have explored.

In fact, you *should* return during the spring. This is especially important if you are unsure whether there are even carp in the water.

Carp spawn during the spring along flooded shorelines where their eggs adhere to submerged shrubs and grasses. You will see them swimming in large groups and splashing wildly in very shallow water. In this way, you will easily be able to determine which spots hold the most, and the largest, fish.

DO NOT give in to the temptation of trying to catch spawning carp! This is one of the first lessons learned by the novice. Spawning carp are not interested in eating. If you only had sex once a year you wouldn't be hungry either.

Spotting Carp

Once you know *where* the carp are, you need to learn *how to find them*. A feeding carp makes a mess, and from the surface you can often see this cloud of suspended mud. This is only a clue, however. In a perfect world it would mark exactly where the fish is, but sometimes it only tells you where it has fed recently. As soon as you spot such a "mud," stop moving and start looking for fish. Carp often feed in shoals (loose groups) and where there is one carp, there may be more. Scan the water all around you. The Ring of Perception is a circle, so don't forget to look behind you.

Underwater the body of a carp appears grey or brown, so at first it may be indistinguishable from rocks or stumps. Since light rays refract as they move between air and water, the fish will also be closer to you than it appears. Try to concentrate on looking for movement. A carp will move smoothly and steadily along the bottom. Be aware that waves on the surface of the water can give the illusion of movement to stationary underwater objects. I once spent fifteen frustrating minutes casting, changing flies, and casting again before Old Master politely asked me why I was trying to hook a car battery.

Carp feed mostly on the bottom. When they see food, they will stop swimming and tilt forward. This points their mouths down towards the food and their tails up towards the surface. If the water is shallow enough, their tails will actually break the surface. Naturally, these fish are called "tailers" and they are a prime target. Spotting a tailing carp is like taking candy from a baby because, unlike their body, the tail of a carp is bright orange or red. Of course, old Master also used to say that disarming a knife-wielding maniac was like taking candy from a baby, so take that with a grain of salt.

So far we have only discussed finding carp with your eyes, but you have other senses too. I am not suggesting that you try to find carp by smell because that's just silly. I *am* suggesting that you practice total awareness when you are fishing. Feel the wind at your back, hear the hawk high above you, taste the sweat on your lip, smell the pine trees on the hill. An old Japanese Master used to say that only by developing your five senses fully will you begin to develop your sixth sense, your "carp-sense." Your carp-sense is your fishing intuition. It is the voice that guides you along the flat, and the tingle that tells you to freeze when a fish is near. When you have reached this level then maybe catching carp *will* be like taking candy from a baby.

FISHING WEAPONS

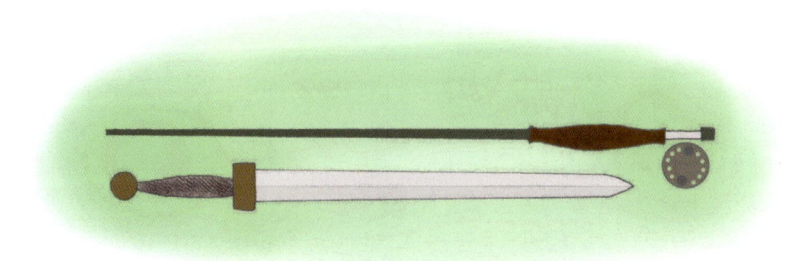

Unless you plan on catching carp with your bare hands while naked, you'll need some gear to help make your fishing excursions more successful.

The Right Gear

Here are the weapons you will need to catch carp on the fly:

1. A decent fly rod, 5 to 8 weight
2. A fly reel with a good drag system
3. Floating fly line, either weight forward or double taper
4. Plenty of backing, 20 lb test or better, and make sure your line to backing knot is strong
5. Tippet material no lighter than 3X and at least a seven foot leader
6. A sturdy landing net, not one of those prissy trout models
7. Polarized sunglasses, the best ones you can get your hands on
8. Comfortable footwear, old sneakers, neoprene booties or whatever you prefer
9. If you need waders, spring for breathable ones – you won't regret it

You Are Smarter Than The Fish.
Or Are You?

All right, now forget everything you have just read. Lists are what you get at strip mall dojos or from "black belt" training DVDs. You say you want to learn Kung-Fu Carp Fishing? Here is another vital concept, so pay attention:

We don't catch fish with hooks or flies or rods or reels. We catch fish with our brains; we catch fish because we are smarter than the fish.

Equipment is only an extension of your technique. If your technique is good, you don't need fancy gear to catch fish and have fun.

"But, but, but..." you will protest, "I saw Old Master in the fly shop the other day buying 9 1/2 foot flourocarbon leaders. Surely he would not have bought them if they weren't essential?"

You should be training instead of snooping into the affairs of others! When Old Master was a young master he tied his own leaders because he was too cheap to buy them. Now he is Old Master with arthritis and bad eyesight so he buys his leaders! When it comes to equipment, don't read too much into what other people say or do. Now, go back and read the brain statement above. Read it again. Read it until you believe it. Read it until you understand it.

While your most important tool is indeed your mind, the list I gave you *is* filled with other good tools. The right gear will make your carp fishing easier and more pleasant. Of course what is right for northern lakes is not necessarily right for urban ponds, and what is right for the student may not be right for the teacher. You must experiment with your fishing to find what works best for you. When it comes to buying equipment, I find the Middle Way of the Buddha to be particularly wise: stay away from crappy WalMart rods *and* over-priced collectors items.

Rods, reels, sunglasses, broadswords, these are the obvious weapons of the carp fisher. But like any respected martial art, Kung-Fu Carp Fishing has its share of secrets which are divulged only to those promising students who have proved their loyalty. Back in the day, Old Master made us lift cauldrons of burning coal with our bare forearms. These days I'd be lucky to get you to wash my car.

Anyway, the secret weapons of Kung-Fu Carp Fishing are subtle because they do not directly aid in catching fish, but rather give the fishing warrior a slight edge over his adversary. When it comes to catching carp, a slight edge can mean the difference between success and being humiliated by a fish.

Preparing Your Body For The Fight

The first secret weapon of Kung-Fu Carp Fishing is feeding yourself correctly. Low blood sugar means fatigue, shakiness, and poor mental function. Be sure to eat well the day before, and bring plenty of moon cakes and yak jerky along when you go fishing.

Water is also a weapon. Actually, water alone is not enough because the real enemy is dehydration, and to fight it you need both water *and* salt. There are lots of sports drinks and snacks (gels, bars) that replenish electrolytes, but water together with any salty snack (like pretzels or peanuts) will do. Again, pre-hydrate the day before you go fishing and bring plenty of water along with you. Dehydration can cause fatigue, headaches, and irritability. I know you hate to take any breaks because you want to spend every possible moment fishing, but if you remember to drink (and eat) often, you will stay sharp and focused longer.

Sleep is a weapon. This is simple. Get a good night's sleep before you fish. A tired angler makes poor decisions, and poor decisions lead to failure.

Finally, sunscreen is a weapon. Sun and water together are a recipe for a bad sunburn which can ruin an otherwise excellent fishing trip. If you plan on fishing several days in a row, consider investing in a hat and a good fishing shirt which will protect your torso and arms from the sun.

If you treat these secret weapons seriously and use them consistently when you fish, your Kung-Fu will improve.

Choosing The Right Weapons

In Kung-Fu Carp Fishing, your fly is the point of your spear, the edge of your blade. It is the business end of your attack so it deserves careful attention. If you have opened a fly fishing magazine recently, you would be forgiven for thinking that catching fish requires three hundred flies in twenty sizes and fifteen different colors, but this is the mindset of the trout fisher. Trout are selective about what they will eat and trout fishers are always trying to "match the hatch" by picking out a fly that imitates as closely as possible what the trout are eating right at that moment. Old Master says that collecting flies is a hobby but catching fish is an art. People accumulate flies because they enjoy it, not because it is necessary. Having an encyclopedia of fly patterns looks impressive but think about this: who would you fear more, the flamboyant knight with all manner of shiny weapons, or the scarred old warrior whose sword is so notched and battered with use that it looks like an old saw? Like the scarred old warrior you need just a few battle proven patterns in your fly box.

Carp are incredibly efficient feeders. Their diet consists mainly of aquatic insects, worms, leeches, crawdads, the occasional baitfish, and freshwater clams which they easily munch with powerful pharyngeal teeth located in their throats. They will also eat popcorn, cheezits, bread crust, and pretty much anything that tastes good to you or me. Because their world is like an all-you-can-eat buffet, carp are not terribly picky. This means that you usually only need a fly that looks edible, not one that resembles any one thing in particular. The best carp flies are those that can suggest several different food items depending on how they are presented.

Since carp feed mostly on the bottom, your flies should be weighted to sink. In water that is at least waist deep use flies tied with a copper or brass bead. This extra weight helps the fly sink down to the fish quickly and the shiny "head" seems to catch their eye. In water less than waist deep, and especially in really skinny water you should switch to a lighter fly because even the tiny splash from a bead-head can spook a sensitive carp. Flies weighted with an underwrapping of thin wire are excellent.

So You Want To Tie Your Own Flies?

If you are anxious to hit the water you can simply stop by your local fly shop and pick up some flies that will work, a handful of woolly buggers will do nicely. But if you want to explore the meditative aspects of Kung-Fu Carp Fishing then you will want to begin by tying your own flies. You can find the "how-to" of fly tying in thousands of books, so I will simply tell you a couple of Kung-Fu fly recipes to try.

The Shaolin Fireball

The Shaolin Fireball is a simple and effective fly for catching carp. You can tie this pattern on any hook that is handy but I like a size #8 or #10 hook - small enough to cast easily but too big for a little bluegill to pick off on a backcast while I'm waiting for a big carp to move into range.

Start by wrapping a layer of thread over the hook shank. Next you need to add some extra weight. A bead-head is fine or you can wrap on some thin wire. If you are a real Kung-Fu monk then you have taken a vow of poverty and can't afford all these speciality items. In that case cut off a short section of paper clip and secure that along the hook shank with more thread. At the rear, tie in a hackle feather. Again, use whatever color is handy. For me that's usually tan or brown. Next, create the body of the fireball. You can tie in chenille and wrap that forward, or you can use any sort of dubbing intended for wet flies. The crucial detail in the Shaolin Fireball is color. The body material you choose should be orange. It can range from day-glow to pumpkin to rust, but it must be orange. It is a mystery why carp respond so well to this color, but Old Master says that a few mysteries make life more interesting. Once you have built up a nice orange body, wind the hackle feather forward and tie it off. Trim the excess and whip finish the head of the fly.

The Little Dragon

The Little Dragon can be tied in any color and in a variety of sizes. Again, I like size #8 or #10 for carp. A Little Dragon tied on a #14 hook makes an excellent bluegill fly.

Start by wrapping a layer of thread over the hook shank. Next, add some weight. The Little Dragon should not be tied with a bead head. It requires either a wrapping of thin wire or attaching a short section of heavy wire like a piece of paper clip along the hook shank with thread. If you have flash then tie in a section at the back of the hook. Next, create the body of the fly. You can use whatever material you have lying around. The color doesn't matter, but you will need rubber legs that match. Be careful to leave plenty of room between the eye of the hook and the body so you can tie in these rubber legs later. If you use flash then wrap that forward around the body and secure it, also well back from the eye. Rubber legs are the key to the Little Dragon; not just their presence but the specific way they are tied on. Choose two equal lengths of rubber legs, longer is better for now because you can always trim them later. Place them side by side on top of the fly so that the fly's head is about halfway between the ends of the legs. Secure the legs with thread so that sections pointing towards the bend of the hook make a narrow "V" over the back of the fly. Next bend the forward sections of the legs so that they are pointing backwards, one on either side of the body. Hold these sections in place with one hand and tie them down with the other. Finally, cover the whole head with a layer of thread and whip finish. There should be four rubber legs extending from the neck of the fly over its back like a dragon's wings. It is another of life's mysteries why carp love rubber legs but this is what makes The Little Dragon such an effective fly.

Dry Flies

When there is an abundance of floating food, carp can often be found sipping or "clooping" it off the surface. Sometimes, just like trout, they will eat insects but they also feed on plant food like mulberries, cottonwood or alder seeds. All an angler needs to do is tie on a floating fly that imitates whatever the carp are eating and cast it gently in front of a feeding fish. The difficulty is that this type of situation is unpredictable because it requires very specific conditions that may last for a week, a day or even just a single afternoon! Despite this, carp can be caught consistently, and through much of the year, on dry flies. The secret lies in locating these hungry fish.

I discovered this secret quite by accident. I found myself at a marina with a waterfront restaurant where patrons regularly throw food to big, eager carp. The establishment was not yet open for the day but the fish were already milling about within an easy cast of shore. Excited by the unexpected opportunity I rigged up my rod but quickly realized that these carp were very particular about what they ate – they only wanted bread. Not only was there nothing in my fly box resembling a piece of floating bread, there were no dry flies of any kind! I tried a dozen other patterns, carp flies, bass flies, trout flies, but nothing worked. I put on a yellow strike indicator (fly fishing's version of a bobber) and tried suspending flies below the surface but I still had no luck.

Adding insult to injury, the fish not only ignored my flies but actually showed interest in my indicator. Every time I made a cast a carp would grab the small plastic sphere and then just as quickly spit it back out. As I watched big fish ignore my fly and try to eat my indicator my frustration slowly gave way to an idea. I pulled in my line and slid the indicator all the way to the end so that the fly dangled just below it. This was a highly non-standard arrangement but now my indicator effectively had a hook. I made another cast and another fish immediately struck, sucking down the indicator and the fly with it. This time I made a quick strip and felt the hook set. I had just caught my first carp on a dry fly!

This experience revealed a new way to catch carp on dry flies but it is also an excellent example of one of the tenents of Kung-Fu Carp Fishing. When I told Old Master how I had caught this carp he nodded and tapped me sharply on the forehead, "Now you know what it means to catch a fish with your mind."

Since then I have witnessed similar scenarios in many places: duck ponds, golf courses and waterfront parks. To scout out your local spots just head down to the water with a loaf of bread and your polarized sunglasses. In no time you will have a fan club of hungry ducks and geese, but look closely and you will likely see carp swimming beneath them. The carp will be busy grabbing anything that gets past the birds, but they may also be competing for food on the surface. Throw a piece of crust out of reach of the birds and you will see it quickly engulfed by a pair of rubbery lips, followed by a swirl of water and the flash of a big orange tail.

These fish are easy to fool with any dry fly that resembles a piece of bread or popcorn. You can tie such flies with traditional materials or you can use a bit of closed cell foam. The most difficult part of catching carp with dry flies is keeping your fly out of the mouths of hungry birds!

BOATS

Wading is a fun and effective way to chase carp, but flats that are surrounded by deep water or bordered by steep cliffs or private property can be inaccessible to a wading angler. The traditional Kung-Fu Carp Fishing technique is to hold your rod in your mouth and swim to such spots but if you have not practiced fighting water moccasins and snapping turtles while treading water, then I suggest that you use a boat. Almost any type of boat can be used to get to an otherwise inaccessible spot. Once you arrive, anchor the boat in shallow water and fish the flat on foot.

Your approach by boat must be stealthy. Zooming into a small bay in a bass boat with a 250HP engine is *not* stealthy. If your boat is motorized, cut the engine as soon as possible. If you have a quiet trolling motor you can use that, but nothing beats a paddle or a push-pole. Also, be very careful when moving around in the boat. Striking or bumping the hull will sound like an explosion to any nearby carp in which case you may as well have used your motor! Even your anchor must be quiet. Lower it slowly and set it gently on the bottom.

Small boats like canoes and kayaks are excellent for this type of fishing. If a flat is a little deeper and the water is above your hips, then wading becomes slow and spotting fish becomes very difficult because of your relatively low vantage point. In this case you will need a boat that is stable enough to stand up in and fish from. This does not mean you need a big boat. In fact, use the smallest boat you can because it will allow you to enter shallower water and to maneuver in tighter spots. The size of the boat you should use depends on your agility and balance. Old Master used to make me fish while balancing on the rails of his canoe. If I fell then I had to swim home! Aluminum jon-boats are the most popular choice, but I personally prefer a sturdy, inflatable, pontoon boat. It is easy to paddle, stable enough to stand on and the soft hull makes it very quiet.

It is easiest to fish from a boat with a comrade. One person maneuvers the boat while the other fishes. The angler can spot fish and verbally direct her partner to move the boat into the best position for a cast. If you fish alone from a boat then you must both steer and fish. If the water is shallow enough to wade you can use the high vantage point of the boat to spot a feeding carp then drop anchor, slip into the water, and pursue the fish on foot. If you want or need to actually cast from the boat then you will need two anchors - one in the bow and one in the stern. When you see a fish, move the boat into position and as quickly as possible lower both anchors before you prepare to make a cast. If you only have one anchor then the wind can swing your boat around, which will either scare the carp or leave you facing the wrong direction!

Boats can be valuable, but they are just another tool. A boat will not make you catch more fish or have more fun. Remember, catching fish depends primarily on your skills and attitude. So before you invest time and money in a boat think very carefully about how you plan to use it and if you really need it.

WADING AND KUNG-FU FOOTWORK

Non-fishermen think wading is just like walking, but unlike walking, wading is a skill that must be practiced and improved. Masters talk about wading as an essential ability. The great Bruce Lee said that, "The quality of a man's technique depends on his footwork, for one cannot use his hands or kicks efficiently until his feet have put him in the desired position." What is true for the hands and feet is also true for nets and fly rods.

How To Stalk Carp

Stalking a tailing carp is like an assassin sneaking through a castle. When the guards appear, the assassin freezes. He becomes part of the wall. When the guards move on, the assassin continues toward the King's chambers. It is the same with stalking a carp. When the carp is tailing, it is intent on feeding and you can approach, but when it pauses and its body returns to a horizontal position you must freeze. The carp is scanning for danger while it chews its food. When it points its nose down for another bite you can again move forward.

It is safest to approach a fish from behind because it cannot see you. However, this puts you in the poorest position to cast from because you need to place your fly in the Ring of Striking, which is in front of the carp's nose. Approaching from the front puts you in the opposite situation. You are in the ideal casting position but the carp is likely to spot you and flee. Approaching from the side is a good compromise. The carp only has one eye pointed in your direction, and you can still place your fly in front of it without casting the line directly over the carp's back (which is a sure way to spook any fish).

Following the wise words of Sun Tzu, "Know your enemy and know yourself," you must not venture onto the water without proper knowledge of your quarry. A novice will advise you to wade very quietly, but Old Master will tell you that this is a load of horse dung. Carp don't have proper ears. They can't hear you, but they can feel you. Every time you move in the water you generate waves – not just the ripples that you see on the surface, but invisible waves travelling through the water in all directions faster than the speed of sound. These waves will dissipate eventually, but if they are too powerful, they will alert the carp to your presence and they will scatter like ninjas in the night.

The carp has no use for an outer ear because the density of its flesh is very close to the density of water. Instead, fish rely on internal organs which intercept the waves and transmit them to an inner ear. In addition, carp, like ninjas, are extra sensitive. They have a structure of fine bones called the Weberian Apparatus which amplifies the waves before they reach the inner ear.

Thus Old Master advises: wade very softly. To catch carp you must learn how to move properly. Otherwise you may as well get a bucket and sit on the bank with the rest of the bait-fishermen. The proper technique for stalking carp is called Shaolin Wading. It is the same technique the Shaolin monks use for meditative walking. Since the Shaolin monks can break metal bars over their heads and are total badasses, you should probably pay attention.

Kung-Fu Footwork

You will say that Shaolin wading looks just like walking in slow motion. I say you wade like a water buffalo! Each time you take a step forward, you must PAUSE. Your front foot should be flat in front of you, and your rear foot should be raised so that only the ball of that foot is in contact with the bottom. Once you have become mindful that your feet are in the proper position, then, and only then may you take the next step. This is the proper technique. Shaolin Wading accomplishes two things simultaneously. First, it forces you to slow down. This is especially important because when you spot a feeding carp, your heart will beat excitedly and you will tend to behave like a fool and wade too quickly. Second, pausing between each step helps you transfer your weight completely to your front foot before you take another step. This prevents you from stumbling or falling, especially over a slippery bottom.

Even if your Shaolin Wading is so good that a carp does not feel you approach, it is still possible that at any moment it might *see* your feet and take off for the next province. Therefore it is often advisable to project a **Cloud of Confusion**. Each time you take a step, after you have transferred your weight to the front foot, but before you have moved your rear foot, wiggle your front toe back and forth a little bit to stir up some mud from the bottom. In this way, you can move forward in a cloud of mud that hides your legs from the eyes of the carp. But beware, because the cloud of confusion is a double edged sword.

The Cloud of Confusion can work too well. To one feeding carp, a moving cloud of mud looks just like another feeding carp. Not only will such a mirage not frighten a hungry fish, it may very well attract it! If this happens and the carp swims too close, it will sense your presence and spook. Also, the cloud of mud you stir up will remain suspended for some time and make it harder for you to see other fish in the area. Like any technique, The Cloud of Confusion has benefits and drawbacks and must be used appropriately to be effective.

VITAL TECHNIQUES

The Basics

Long ago there was a boy whose father was a simple farmer. In their village lived a *ronin*, a masterless samurai. This ronin was a drunkard and a lout, but he was strong and he bullied and terrorized the villagers for fun. Late one evening the boy's father and the ronin had occasion to pass one another in the street. In his drunkeness, the ronin took insult at the farmer's perceived lack of respect, and with a vicious cry drew his blade and decapitated the man.

The farmer's son was devastated and outraged and he vowed to avenge his father. The next morning the boy packed his clothes and hiked into the mountains above the village to a small temple. The old monk who lived in the temple was a master swordsman but had long retired from the life of the blade. He listened to the boy's story and thought for a time. Finally he rose and motioned the boy to follow. The old monk produced a *bokken*, a wooden practice sword. In the courtyard he showed the boy how to make the most basic strike: the straight, overhead cut. When the boy had made several practice cuts, the master nodded his approval and told the boy to make one thousand cuts. After one thousand cuts, the boy's hands were blistered and swollen, his legs and arms fatigued and shaking. He went inside where the old monk traded the *bokken* for a broom and gave the boy a list of chores to complete before nightfall.

The next day was the same. The boy made one thousand overhead cuts in the courtyard and spent the rest of his day doing chores. Every day for one year, standing in the snow or rain or sun he swung the *bokken* a thousand times. At the end of one year the boy was eager to improve his skills, so he approached his master,

"Master, it has been one year, may I learn a new technique?"

The old master frowned. "No. Go and make one thousand cuts."

The boy bowed deeply and returned to the courtyard with his *bokken*.

At the end of the second year the boy's hands were tough, his arms were lean and strong. He went to his master again, "Master, I have practiced the overhead cut one thousand times every day for two years. Will you teach me a new technique?"

The master leaned forward and looked closely at the boy. "No. Go and make one thousand cuts."

Disappointed, but resolved to avenge his father, the boy returned to the courtyard with his *bokken*.

After three years and more than one million cuts, the boy went to his master a third time, "Master, it has been three years. May I learn a new technique?"

The old master smiled. "No. You are ready. Go and take your revenge."

The next day the boy took his bokken and hiked down the mountain to his village. He found the ronin in the town square, drinking a bottle of *sake*. The boy raised his wooden sword towards the burly warrior. The ronin laughed loudly. "What do you want, boy?"

"You killed my father. I am here to take my revenge," the boy replied nervously.

The ronin snarled and tossed his bottle aside. He stood up and drew his long sword. "So you want to die too?"

Without thinking the boy struck. With one strong, swift, overhead cut he cracked the ronin's skull, killing him instantly.

In this way, fly fishing is the same as swordmanship. You don't need fancy tricks, no spinning back casts or jumping roll casts. You simply need to make a reasonably straight cast at the moment when it matters, so practice the basics as much as possible. Remember, the measure of a good cast is not in feet; **the only good cast is the one that catches a fish**. It is fine to learn new casts and to improve distance, as long as it is done with proper intent - to catch more carp!

The Strike

Striking is the core of Kung-Fu Carp Fishing. The strike is the pivotal moment when the mental battle is won and the physical battle commences. It is also exciting as hell! The best presentation is to gently cast your fly into the Ring of Striking and let it sink naturally, right in front of the carp. The difficulty with this natural presentation is that you probably will not feel the strike. Carp do not actually bite. Instead they literally suck food into their mouths. The inhalation and rejection of a fly by a carp is as gentle as a breath, and often very quick. Therefore, with a naturally sinking presentation it is essential that you can see the carp.

Just as a fighter trains to read the opponent's movements – the smallest twitch, the slightest telegraph before a punch – you must also train to read the body language of a carp. As your fly sinks, look for the carp to accelerate or change direction, even a tiny bit. After that, the fish will pause suddenly, and often it will tilt its head down a bit.

WHAT ARE YOU WAITING FOR, GRASSHOPPER? SET THE HOOK!

Some people will tell you to set the hook with a quick strip-strike, others will say to gently lift your rod into the fish. I don't care how you set the hook. The fact of the matter is that it doesn't matter what I tell you, because in the heat of the moment you are going to do the same thing you've always done! So if it's been working, don't try to fix it.

Drawing Your Prey

As your casting accuracy improves, you can begin to *draw* the carp. Drawing means feinting or leaving an opening that entices your opponent to react or attack in a certain way. For example, if you cast your fly in front and just to the side of a carp, you force it to both turn *and* accelerate, giving you exactly the signal you need to set the hook in time.

Sometimes you need to make an active retrieve. If the fish is moving beneath overhanging bushes or if there is an obstacle between you and the fish, you will have to lead it. Carefully study the carp's movement and try to predict where it is headed. Make your cast and begin your retrieve so that your fly intercepts the fish's path at just the right moment. You can use either a slow or a moderately fast retrieve. Carp don't like to sprint, but they will swim after a tasty looking morsel.
One nice thing about an active retrieve is that you *will* be able to feel the take and often the hook sets itself.

Seeing Without Seeing

Another time you will need an active retrieve is when you cannot actually see the fish. I don't mean blind-casting. Blind-casting for carp is a fools errand. I am talking about the art of seeing without seeing.

By now you are wondering if I've been hitting the fire-water, but I assure you that I am not blowing smoke. When the water is too turbid for sight-fishing and you can't actually see the fish, you don't need to pack up and go home, you just need to know what to look for.

Once you have spotted a mud cloud, continue to scan the area carefully. If the water is shallow enough, look for tails sticking out of the water. Sometimes you will see the water boiling as a carp undulates it's tail just below the surface. If the water is too deep for this then you need to look for bubbles. Decomposing matter and frog farts create gasses that are trapped in the muck. When a carp disturbs the bottom, the gasses are released and rise to the surface in the form of small bubbles.

When you see any of these signs – tails, boiling water, or bubbles – *then* you know where the carp is. Cast past the fish and retrieve your fly through the area where it's feeding. With a little luck, the carp will be facing the right way and will take your offering.

The Heron Technique

The Heron technique is to carp fishing what Wing Chun trapping is to in-fighting. It is a powerful, close-range technique that requires nerves of steel to apply successfully.

Often, in turbid water or in low-light conditions, you may not spot a fish until you have stumbled into the Ring of Shadows. Since you are now too close for a traditional cast, it is time to employ the Heron Technique.

First, using Shaolin Wading, you must approach to within

one rod length of the carp. Do this slowly and carefully, but with total commitment to your course of action. If the bottom is muddy, you can also project a Cloud of Confusion. If the bottom is gravel then wade extra softly, for the clack of even tiny pebbles at this distance can scare a fish.

During your approach, you must hold your rod out *toward* the carp. Many novices will sneak up on a carp with their rod pointing backwards because they don't want to frighten the fish with their rod tip. But let me ask you this: does the heron stalk its prey with its beak hidden beneath its wing? No. The heron knows that his best chance is with his weapon ready, and the same is true for you. After all, what do you think will happen when the novice is standing over the fish and *then* swings his rod into position?

You should have only a few feet of your leader outside the rod tip, about as many feet as the water is deep. In your free hand, hold enough line to get your leader just past the guides. When you are within a rod length of the carp, stop and wait until the carp stops feeding and its head comes up. When it begins to move forward ever so slightly, then let your fly sink naturally just in front of the fish's head. As soon as the carp spots your offering it will quickly engulf it. Set the hook by lifting your rod tip straight up and then *point the rod in the direction the fish runs*. This will allow the carp to safely take the leader to line knot through the guides while you control the speed with your off hand. Once the line is clear you can smoothly lift your rod and play the fish off the reel. Good job, Grasshopper!

Fishing Like The Old Master

When Old Master fights a big carp there is no doubt who will win. It always appears that he knows what the fish will do before the fish itself knows! Such perfection of skill only comes from a lifetime of training. There is an old saying that a journey of a thousand miles begins with a single step. Thus, even though you should aspire to reach that high level of skill, you must start with the basics.

As soon as a carp feels the hook it will make an explosive run. Immediately clear any slack line with your free hand. Clearing the line means keeping it free of tangles and controlling it between your thumb and forefinger as the carp pulls it out. If you let go of the slack or if there are any tangles, the line will tighten abruptly and the fish will snap your tippet.

Once the slack line has been cleared you can proceed to play the fish off of the reel. The drag should be set well below the breaking point of your tippet but it should be set high enough so that the carp has to work to take line off of the spool.

The position of your rod during the fight is very important. If you point your rod directly at the fish, you would be using only the reel to fight it. Holding your rod vertically puts all the stress on the tip which could break it. The best position is somewhere in between. This allows the tip to act as a shock absorber but transfers the stress down to the thick portions of the rod. It also minimizes friction on the line while maximizing leverage.

Watch where the fish runs to. If it heads into deeper water, let it go. If it swims towards cover, like a submerged log, you will need to steer it away. Since you have scouted the area, you should already know where these underwater hazards are. To steer a fish, simply rotate your rod to the left or the right. Do not raise or lower the tip, just rotate it to one side. This will pull the fish's head slightly off line and cause it veer away from its desired destination.

A bonefish will end up as shark food if it is exhausted during the fight so it is important to play them aggressively and land them as soon as possible. A grown carp, however, has very few predators and provided it is revived sufficiently it will be able to rest safely in deeper water. So take your time with the fight. Be flexible, like a stalk of bamboo in the wind. When the carp pulls, you yield, and when it slows you begin to bring it back. The battle will sway back and forth and you will win only by being patient and going with the flow.

Landing The Carp

When you play a carp, it is the fish that decides when the battle is over. Once the carp has determined that you are a worthy opponent, it will surface and roll onto its side to signal that you have prevailed. If you have a net, you should already have it in the water and in position! Sticking the net in the water at the last moment is a rookie move and the carp will reward you with a splash in the face and another run. Get the fish's head into your net – it's all right if the net isn't big enough for the whole fish. Carp are heavier on the front end so scooping them up head first prevents them from flopping out of your net.

If you don't have a net, you have two options. First, if you are on or near shore you can literally "land" the fish. Simply pull it gently out of the water and onto land. With a heavier fish you will only be able to beach part of it, so it is essential that you drop your rod and leap on the fish with the speed of a mantis before it rolls back into the water.

If you do not have a net and you are not near shore, you will have to attempt the advanced technique of Whispering.

Whispering

Using one hand to play the fish with the rod, extend your free hand towards the fish, palm up like you are offering a gift. As you draw the fish near to your open hand whisper calmly to it. What a carp whisperer says to their fish is a closely guarded secret and you must develop your own spiel. If the fish freaks out, you've said something wrong.

Gently slide your open hand under the fish, near the pectoral fin. Remember that the carp has rolled onto its side by now. Leave it that way. On its side it will stay calm and relaxed as if in a trance. If you right it, it will regain its senses and try to break your tippet.

As you lift the carp from the water, still whispering to it, stash your rod in your armpit and use your other hand to lightly grasp the fish just in front of its tail. Carp are slippery and not conducive to handling, but the most secure way to hold one is with one hand supporting its belly and the other gently (but firmly) wrapped just in front of its tail. Now you can pose for a quick photo. Do not remove the fly until the picture is taken. That way, if your prize catch thrashes free you can bring it back to hand! Also, make sure the light is behind the picture taker; if you take a backlit photo then don't expect Old Master to include it in the annual Kung-Fu Carp Fishing newsletter.

After a photo or two, remove your fly and lower the fish back into the water. If the carp is especially tired, rock it back and forward to help move some water over its gills. Even if it protests, don't release it until it shows you that it has recovered substantially. When it has, send it off toward deeper water where it can rest and recover in safety.

The Most Important Thing

You have learned the techniques of Kung-Fu Carp Fishing, and now you are ready to learn its final tenet: *Have Fun*.

This is not as simple as it sounds because fishing is most fun when you are catching fish. So you must take all of your new skills and practice them. Go fishing. A lot. Eventually your own personal style of Kung-Fu Carp Fishing will evolve. You will adopt new techniques and adapt old ones to new situations. You will catch fish, and you will have fun. You will begin to yearn for the dog days of summer when the sun is high and the big carp are cruising the shallows. You will also become that rogue angler, the one who the trout fishers all think is a little nuts. But if you persevere despite their critical glances, someday you may unite with the other rogue anglers of the world to elevate the mighty carp to its rightful status as the most worthy opponent that swims in fresh water.

This is the knowledge of Kung-Fu Carp Fishing as Old Master taught it to me. His wish was that I would take his knowledge and that some day my skills would surpass his. This goal still eludes me but like him, it is my sincere hope that you will develop your own skills so that someday you too may become a Master in your own right. For now, go forth and wade softly.

About The Author

Adam Dailey-McIlrath has been fishing and training in the martial arts since he was a boy. He has earned a living as a sushi chef, a shark feeder, a deckhand, a math tutor, and a police officer.

Adam enjoys many different types of angling. He has caught more than 50 different species of freshwater and saltwater fish, but his greatest passion is catching carp on the fly.

Adam's writing has been published in *The Drake* magazine and on the Tenkara USA website. Stories of his fishing and world travels can be found on his blog at **FishingDojo.com**.

Adam holds a Masters degree in Mathematics and a black belt in Aikido. He currently lives and fishes in Honolulu, Hawaii.

Printed in Great Britain
by Amazon